GRASSLAND MAMMALS

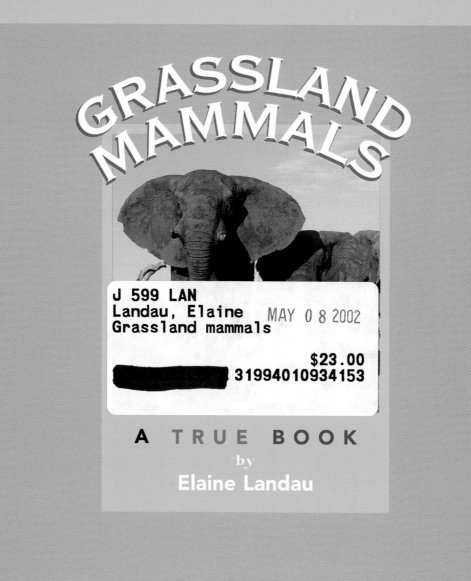

A TRUE BOOK

by

Elaine Landau

Children's Press®
A Division of Grolier Publishing
New York London Hong Kong Sydney
Danbury, Connecticut

For Michael, whose smile is like sunshine on the prairie

Reading Consultant
Linda Cornwell
Learning Resource Consultant
Indiana Department of
Education

Subject Consultant
Kathy Carlstead, Ph.D.
National Zoological Park
Smithsonian Institution

A red kangaroo gets
ready to leap.

Library of Congress Cataloging-in-Publication Data

Landau, Elaine.
    Grassland mammals / by Elaine Landau.
        p. cm. — (A true book)
    Summary: Briefly describes such animals as giraffes, prairie dogs,
and elephants that live on the grasslands, prairies, and tropical savannas around the world.
    ISBN 0-516-20039-9 (lib. bdg.)   ISBN 0-516-26099-5 (pbk.)
    1. Grassland animals—Juvenile literature. [1. Grassland animals.]
    I. Title. II. Series.
QL115.3.L35   1996
599—dc20   96-3892
                                           CIP
                                         AC

Contents

Grasslands are often the border between dry deserts and heavy forests.

Grasslands

Picture a seemingly endless sea of grass, stretching like a thick green carpet across the land. These vast grassy areas are known as grasslands. They can be found on every continent on Earth.

The two types of grasslands are steppes and prairies.

Steppes, found in parts of North America, Europe, and Asia, are usually hot, dry places. Short grasses grow there because there is little rain.

Prairies exist in moister areas. Tall grasses cover the land like a green blanket. In some places, prairie grasses grow several feet high. Prairies are found in North and South America, Africa, Europe, and New Zealand.

A tropical savanna

Some people regard the
tropical savannas in Africa,
South America, Asia, India,
and Australia as a third type
of grassland. A variety of

The grasslands of the plains are home to many interesting mammals.

coarse grasses and some scattered trees and shrubs grow in these regions. Savanna grasses crop up in broad patches, however, and do not cover the land completely.

This book introduces a few interesting mammals of the grasslands. Mammals are animals with backbones and with larger brains than other types of animals. They are also the only animals that nurse their young. Unfortunately, due to overhunting and the destruction of their habitat, as grasslands are turned into farms, many grassland mammals have become endangered.

NORTH AMERICA

E

Saha
Dese

Prairie dogs live in western North America.

CENTRAL AMERICA

A F

SOUTH AMERICA

African elephants live in Africa south of the Sahara Desert.

N

W   E

S

A N T A

OPE

ASIA

CA

Aardvarks are found in Africa south of the Sahara Desert.

Giraffes in the wild are found in East Africa south of the Sahara Desert. They also now live in the area's national parks and game preserves.

AUSTRALIA

Kangaroos are found in Australia and neighboring islands.

TICA

The mighty African elephant

African Elephants

The dark gray African elephant is the world's largest land animal. The male weighs about 12,000 pounds (5,443 kilograms), while the smaller female weighs about 7,000 pounds (3,175 kg). Nearly everything about this animal is big. Its huge ears are about

4 feet (1.2 meters) wide. Its ivory tusks—two long, curved upper teeth—weigh up to 100 pounds (45 kg) each. Even the elephant's loosely hanging wrinkled skin weighs nearly 2,000 pounds (907 kg).

Elephants are often on the move in search of food and do not stay in one place for very long. They eat grasses, some types of bushes and leaves, green nuts, and ripe fruits that have fallen from

Despite their enormous size, elephants walk at a brisk rate of about 4 miles (6.4 km) per hour.

trees. In a single day, an elephant can easily eat from 300 to 500 pounds (136 to 227 kg) of food.

African elephants are quite intelligent. They live in herds of fifteen to thirty animals

Each day, an elephant drinks up to 25 gallons (95 liters) of water.

and make a broad range of sounds to communicate with one another. Researchers believe that elephants also have excellent memories as well, and may experience a number of emotions.

Elephants have been known to rescue other elephants trapped by hunters and have saved humans from an angry member of their herd.

Their tremendous size and powerful strength protect

them from most predators, but sometimes lions kill and eat elephant calves. Through the years, however, humans have become the greatest

Lions are dangerous to young elephant calves.

In many areas, elephants are now protected by law, but regulations are not always obeyed. An illegal ivory trade still exists.

threat to the elephant's survival. Hunted and overkilled for their valuable ivory tusks, the world's population of elephants has decreased sharply.

Prairie Dogs

The prairie dog—a member of the squirrel family—is a light brown furry animal whose cry sounds like a dog's bark. They are about 12 inches (30 centimeters) tall with a tail about 3 inches (7.6 centimeters) long.

The two major types of prairie dogs are the black-tailed

A prairie dog listens for a predator (left). Prairie dogs live in colonies (above).

prairie dog and the less common white-tailed one. Both kinds are extremely social. They live in groups of hundreds or even thousands, known as colonies or towns.

Prairie dogs make their homes in burrows, which they dig as deep as 16 feet (5 m) below ground. Each burrow usually has two openings so that the animal can escape if it is threatened by a predator, such as a ferret, eagle, coyote, or bobcat. Many burrows have a mound of dirt around the entrance. These mounds serve as lookout points, allowing a prairie dog to see an enemy

Prairie dogs climb out of their underground burrow.

approaching. Prairie dogs
only leave their burrows
during the day to look for
grass, roots, seeds, and green
plants to eat. Outside, if the
prairie dog becomes aware
of danger, it warns the others

in the colony by making a loud chirping sound.

Farmers and ranchers have disliked prairie dogs because they suspected that these animals ate grass and plants needed by their livestock. They were also concerned that their animals might accidentally stumble into a burrow and injure their legs. But research has not shown that prairie dogs pose any real threat to livestock.

A prairie dog nibbles on grass.

A giraffe's long
neck has only
seven bones—
the same as
a human's.

Giraffes

What do you notice first about a giraffe? Its height is certainly unusual. Giraffes are the tallest animals on earth. Males grow to about 18 feet (5.5 m) tall. Females, at about 14 feet (4.3 m) tall, are somewhat smaller.

Much of the giraffe's height comes from its long legs and

A giraffe munches the tops of trees.

neck. Its neck allows the giraffe to reach high into the trees for leaves, shoots, and fruits to eat. The giraffe's long legs also serve the animal well—enabling it to run far and fast. Giraffes can reach speeds of up to 34 miles (55 kilometers) an hour.

The reddish brown patches on the giraffe's coat are special too. In a way, these

Giraffes on the move

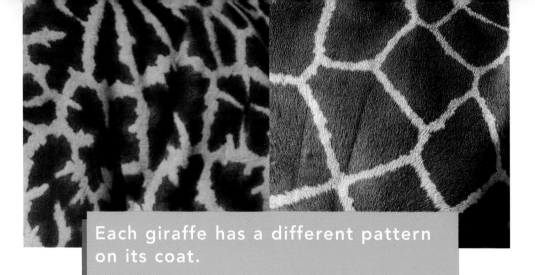

Each giraffe has a different pattern on its coat.

markings are like human fingerprints. Each giraffe has its own pattern, and—while the markings darken with age—their shape never changes. This means that researchers can identify individual giraffes in the wild and study them over time.

Lions and hyenas are the giraffe's main enemies. If a

giraffe escapes from a lion's grip, it can nearly always outrun it. If it is forced to fight, the giraffe defends itself by kicking with its strong legs and hard hooves. These powerful blows can kill.

Hyenas sometimes attack giraffes when the giraffes reach down to eat grass or feed on a low branch.

Giraffes have been hunted for their unique hides.

Humans have not always been the giraffe's friend. At times, giraffes have been widely hunted. And these animals have lost much of their territory as grasslands have been turned into farms.

Aardvarks

The aardvark is a short, stout African animal whose name means "earth pig." It stands about 3 feet (90 cm) high and weighs in at 120 pounds (54 kg). The aardvark has a long narrow head, a piglike snout, and ears that look like a donkey's ears. Aardvarks have gray or pinkish skin, but they usually look brown because their bodies are nearly always covered with crusty soil.

Aardvarks live in underground burrows that they dig

Aardvarks are known as "earth pigs."

Aardvarks dig with their claws, so they are often covered with soil.

with their claws. They are fast diggers and can quickly dig a hole to hide in if an enemy is nearby.

The aardvark also uses its claws to destroy ant and

This aardvark is hunting for an ant or termite nest.

termite nests. Once it opens a nest, the aardvark sweeps up the insects with its long, sticky tongue.

These animals have keen hearing. When out alone searching for food, an aardvark listens for approaching predators. If it senses danger, it retreats to its burrow. But if flight is impossible, it rolls over on its back and defends itself with its claws. Lions, leopards, hunting dogs, and pythons prey on aardvarks. Some African tribes also hunt these animals for their meat.

A young aardvark already has a large snout.

Kangaroos

Did you know that there are many different kinds of kangaroos? Most people think of this animal as looking like the 6-foot (1.8-m) tall, 180-pound (82-kg) red kangaroo. But the gray kangaroo is almost as big. There is also a 16-inch (41-cm) long rat kangaroo—

An eastern gray kangaroo

one of the smallest members
of the kangaroo family.

All kangaroos are marsupials,
mammals whose babies grow
in a pouch on their mother's
belly. A newborn red or gray
kangaroo is tiny. It is blind,
hairless, and weighs less than

A young kangaroo lives in its mother's pouch.

1 ounce (28 grams). Shortly after birth, the little kangaroo climbs into the mother's pouch. It spends the next few months of its life there, drinking its mother's milk while it continues to grow. Later on, the young kangaroo, called a

joey, leaves the pouch for short periods to explore the outside world.

Adult kangaroos feed on grasses and other plants. They usually spend the hot daylight hours resting in the shade and look for food at night. At times, large numbers of

A kangaroo feeds on plants.

kangaroos, known as mobs, gather together where food is plentiful.

Perhaps kangaroos are best known for the unusual way they move about. They hop on their strong hind legs. A large kangaroo can reach speeds of up to 30 miles (48 km) an hour. If necessary, it can jump as far as 28 feet (8.5 m) in a single bound.

The kangaroo's main predator is a wild dog, called

Dingoes are wild dogs of Australia (above). Sheep ranchers once killed kangaroos, but laws protect these unique animals today (right).

a dingo. Eagles and foxes also frequently attack young joeys. In the past, humans killed large numbers of kangaroos for their hides. Today, the kangaroo is legally protected throughout Australia.

To Find Out More

Here are more places to learn about grassland mammals:

Books

Catchpole, Clive. **Grasslands.** Dial Books, 1984.

Darling, Kathy. **Kangaroos on Location.** Lothrop, Lee & Shepard, 1993.

Dewey, Jennifer. **Animal Architecture.** Orchard Books, 1991.

Dorros, Arthur. **Elephant Families.** HarperCollins, 1994.

Hirschi, Ron. **Who Lives on the Prairie?** G.P. Putnam, 1989.

Patent, Dorothy Hinshaw. **Prairie Dogs.** Clarion, 1993.

Staub, Frank J. **America's Prairies.** Carolrhoda Books, 1994.

Organizations

African Wildlife Foundation
1717 Massachusetts Avenue, NW
Washington, DC 20036
(202) 265-8393
http://www.rhinochasers. com/awf/index.html

Sierra Club
730 Polk Street
San Francisco, CA 94109
(415) 776-2211
http://www.sierraclub.org/

Smithsonian: National Zoological Park
3000 block of Connecticut Avenue, NW
Washington, DC 20008
(202) 673-4800
http://www.si.sgi.com/perspect.afafam/afazoo.html

Mammals of Africa.
ZooGuide's Library.
Walk with African elephants, giraffes, lions, zebras, and more.
Ages 7+

The San Diego Zoo Presents: The Animals!
The Software Toolworks.
Explore every part of this zoo as you see and learn about your favorite animals in this CD-ROM.
Ages 7+

African Elephant
http://www.aza.org/aza/ssp/afriele.html
Learn about this giant animal's habitat, diet, and behavior, as well as threats to its survival.

Australian A-Z Animal Archive
http://aaa.com.au/A-Z.html
Discover every animal in Australia—from antechinus to zyzomys.

Giraffe Cam
http://www.ceram.com/cheyenne/giraffe.html
Watch giraffes at the Cheyenne Mountain Zoo— live on your computer!

Prairie Dogs
http://pages.prodigy.com/pdogs/pdog.html
Learn about these smart, playful, and hard-working animals.

Important Words

burrow a hole in the ground made by an animal for shelter

continent one of the seven great land masses on earth

calves newborn young

endangered at risk of dying out

habitat an animal's environment

herd a group of animals

livestock farm animals

marsupial an animal whose young grow in a pouch on the mother's belly

predator an animal that lives by hunting other animals

prey an animal hunted by another for food

shrub a thick low-growing bush

tusks an elephant's long, curved ivory teeth

Index

Meet the Author

Elaine Landau worked as a newspaper reporter, children's book editor, and youth services librarian before becoming a full-time writer. She has written more than ninety books for young people.

Her favorite grassland animal is the African elephant. She has long admired this mammal's remarkable memory.